Weather

FaQ

Frequently asked Questions

Written by Valerie Wyatt

Illustrated by Brian Share

Kids Can Press

For Jennifer, Stephanie, Matthew and Amanda, great nephew and nieces all

Acknowledgments

Like every book, this one was a co-operative effort. It began years ago when my glider-flying husband, Larry MacDonald, got me interested in the ways of weather. Valerie Hussey and Ricky Englander published my first book on the subject, *Weatherwatch*, back in 1990 and pushed for a new book with an updated look and feel. Dr. Robert Schemenauer read the manuscript and checked it for meteorological accuracy. Marie Bartholomew gave the book its unique look and skillfully brought together words and art. I thank them all. Most of all, I thank my friend and editor Liz MacLeod who, in her care for the manuscript (and for her authors), is a tribute to her profession.

Kids Can Press acknowledges the support of the Ontario Arts Council, the Canada Council for the Arts and the Government of Canada, through the BPIDP, for our publishing activity.

Published in Canada by
Kids Can Press Ltd.
29 Birch Avenue
Toronto, ON M4V 1E2

Published in the U.S. by
Kids Can Press Ltd.
4500 Witmer Estates
Niagara Falls, N.Y. 14305-1386

Edited by Elizabeth MacLeod
Designed by Marie Bartholomew

Cover designed by Marie Bartholomew and David Barkworth
Printed in Hong Kong by Wing King Tong Co. Ltd.

CM 00 0 9 8 7 6 5 4 3 2 1
CM PA 00 0 9 8 7 6 5 4 3 2 1

Canadian Cataloguing in Publication Data

Wyatt, Valerie
Weather

(Frequently asked questions)
Includes index.

ISBN 1-55074-582-4 (bound) ISBN 1-55074-815-7 (pbk.)

1. Weather – Miscellanea – Juvenile literature. I. Share, Brian. II Title. III. Series.

QC981.3.W92 2000 j551.5 C99-932402-0

Kids Can Press is a Nelvana company

Contents

Cool It!

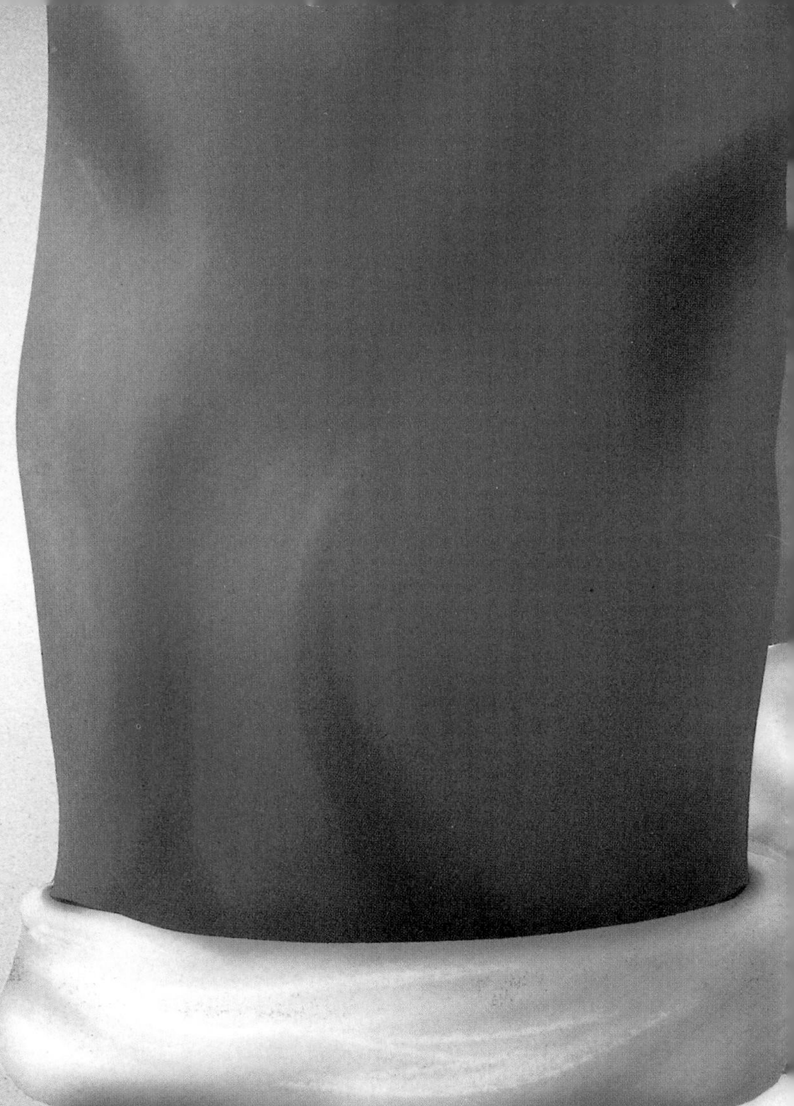

Picture this. It's hot enough to fry an egg on the sidewalk. The Sun is beating down, making your skin prickle, and you've downed so much lemonade your lips feel permanently puckered. Now the soles of your sneakers are starting to melt. What you need is a COLD button to push for a blast of arctic air.

Sorry, but so far no one has figured out how to chill out a scorcher or turn off a blizzard. The weather is out of our control. Rain wipes out picnics, the wind screams through branches like a toddler with a toothache, tornadoes rip off roofs, and thunderclouds spit out hail bigger than baseballs.

What makes the weather so hot, cold and weird? Read on for answers to your Frequently Asked Questions about weather.

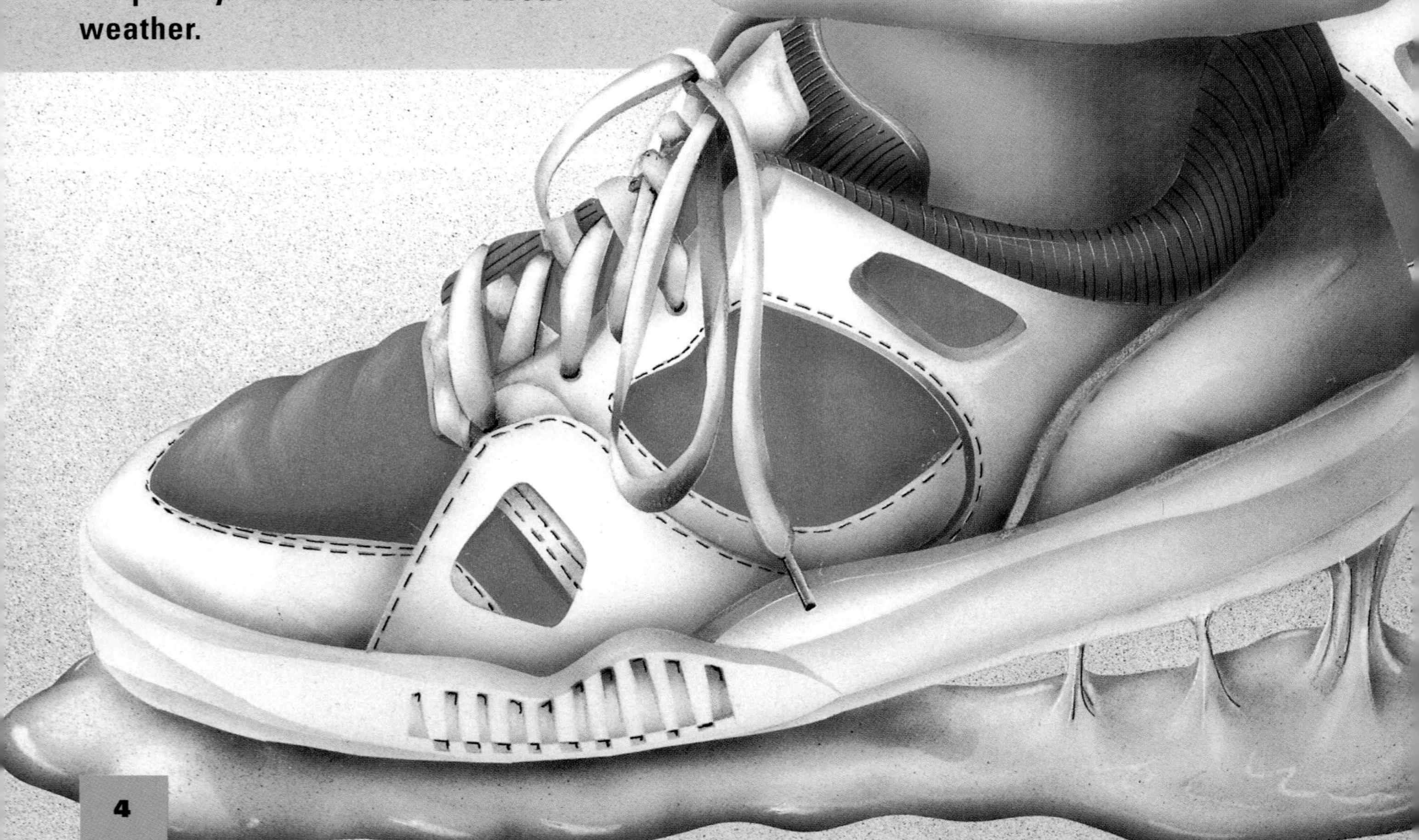

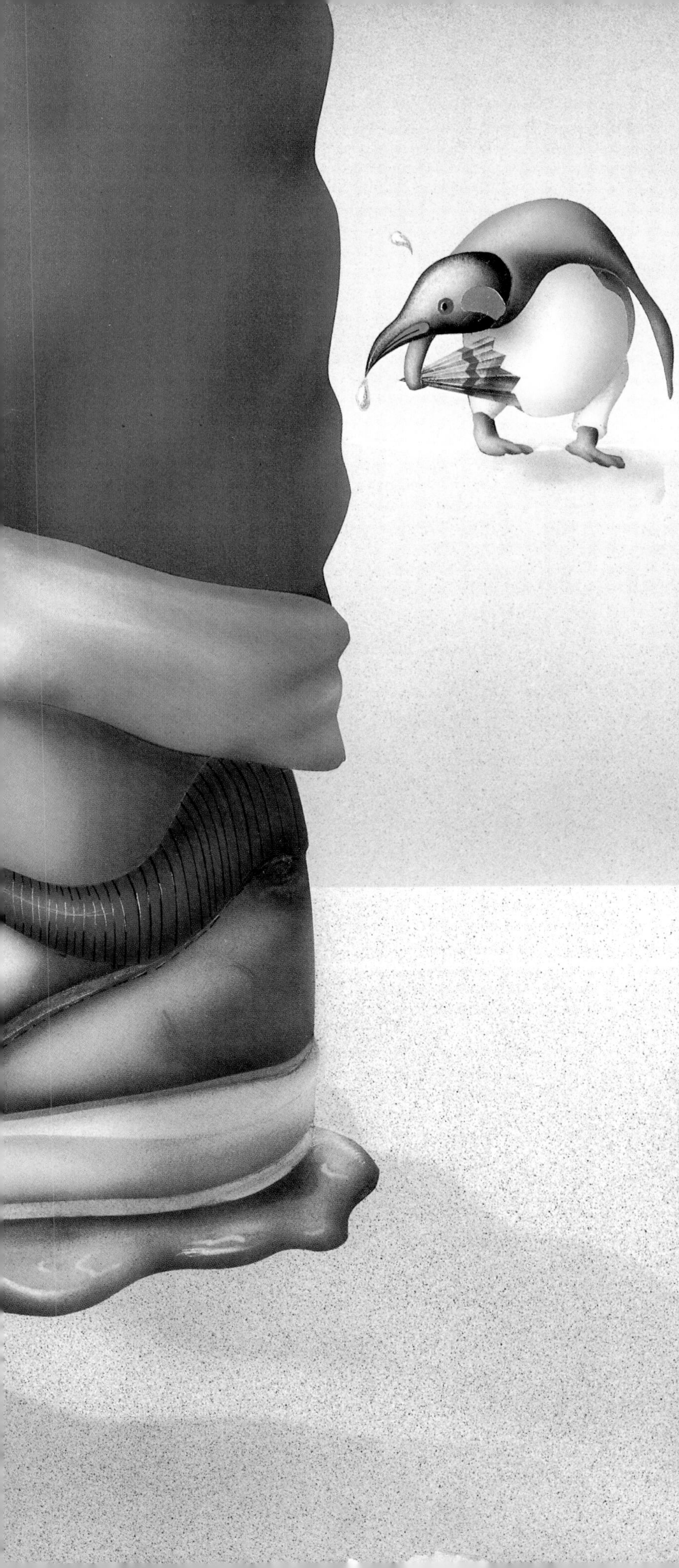

FaQ

Does it ever really get hot enough to fry an egg on the sidewalk?

When a heat wave struck Grimsby, Ontario, on July 9, 1936, driving the temperature up to 42°C (108°F), people decided to find out. They cracked an egg on a hot patch of sidewalk and sat back in the shade to watch. In just seven minutes the egg was fried.

Most days hot sidewalks are cooled by the air above them. On this hot July day, however, the air was just too hot to do any cooling. With the Sun beaming down, the sidewalk became like a frying pan. Now that's what you'd call sunny-side up.

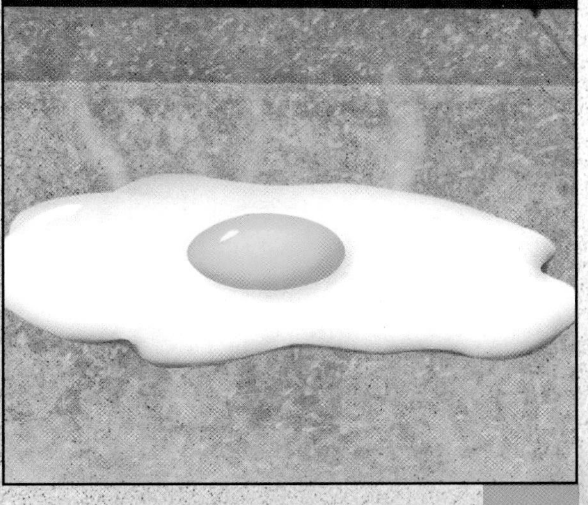

Brrrrrr and Shiverrrrr!

FAQ

How hot and cold can it get?

Here are the record holders.

+58°C (136.4°F)
The hottest temperature ever recorded, at Al'aziziyah, Libya

+15°C (59°F)
The average temperature on Earth

–89.2°C (–128.6°F)
The coldest temperature ever recorded, at Vostok, Antarctica

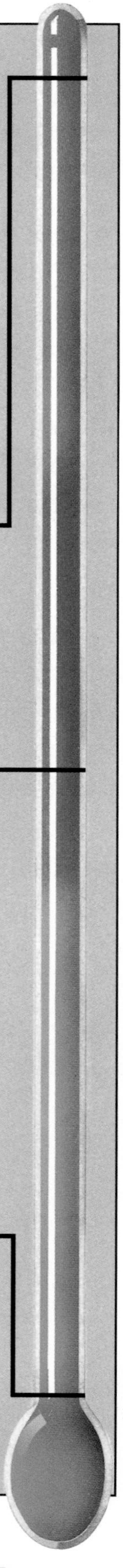

FAQ

Why is it so hot in some places and so cold in others?

Whether you freeze or fry depends on a lot of things. How close you live to the equator, for one. The closer you are, the warmer the weather will generally be because the equator gets the Sun's rays more directly for more of the year than anywhere else on Earth.

If you live near a huge body of water, such as an ocean or a very large lake, your weather will have fewer extreme temperatures than if you were landlocked. That's because water can absorb heat in summer or give off heat in winter and even change wind patterns.

Mountains can make the weather wetter — or drier — than nearby areas. When warm, moist winds sweep up the side of a mountain, clouds form and rain falls. On the other side of the mountain it may be desert-like.

From day to day, there can also be big changes as huge masses of air that are cool or warm, wet or dry, glide overhead. These huge blobs of air are created as the Sun beams down, warming some parts of Earth and the air above it more than others. The blobs cruise overhead, bumping into one another. When one air mass pushes another out of the way, the weather usually changes soon after.

Winds and ocean currents such as those related to El Niño can also make a big difference. Even cities can affect the weather. Buildings and pavement trap heat, making cities as much as 5°C (9°F) warmer than the surrounding countryside. So where you live has a lot to do with how hot or cold — and how rainy or dry — it is.

Snowsuit or Swimsuit?

FaQ

How can you tell if the weather is about to change?

When a new air mass pushes out an old one, expect a change in the weather. Hot, sunny days may be replaced by cool, wet ones. Or a storm may blow in.

How can you tell when a new air mass is overhead? Check a barometer, a device that measures air pressure. When the needle on the barometer jumps up or down, it means that the air mass over the barometer has changed and that means the weather will change.

Here's how to make a simple barometer and see for yourself.

Byte

On January 10, 1911, the temperature in Rapid City, South Dakota, dropped 26°C (47°F) in 15 minutes. Quick — grab a sweater. And another one. And another ...

You'll need

a balloon
a jar with a wide mouth
an elastic band
a drinking straw
scissors, tape, a piece of paper, a pencil

1. Blow up the balloon, then let the air out. Cut the balloon in half and throw out the part with the neck. Stretch the other part over the mouth of the jar and hold it in place with the elastic band. Make sure the seal is airtight.

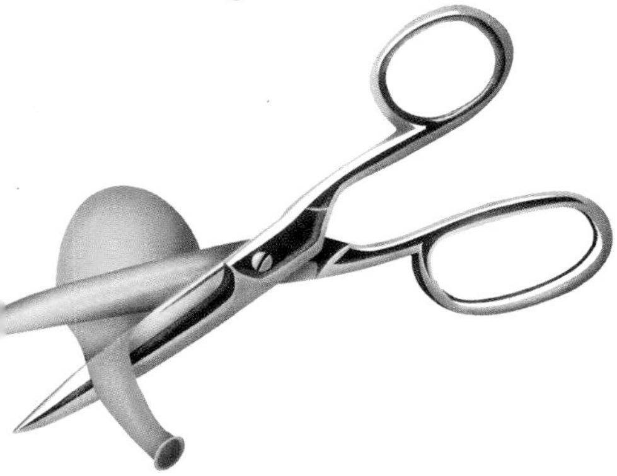

2. Tape the straw in place as shown.

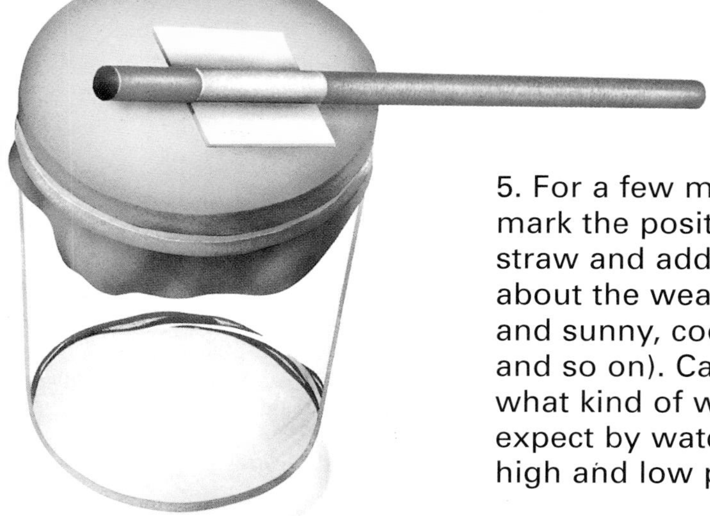

3. Set the jar next to a wall and tape up the piece of paper beside it.

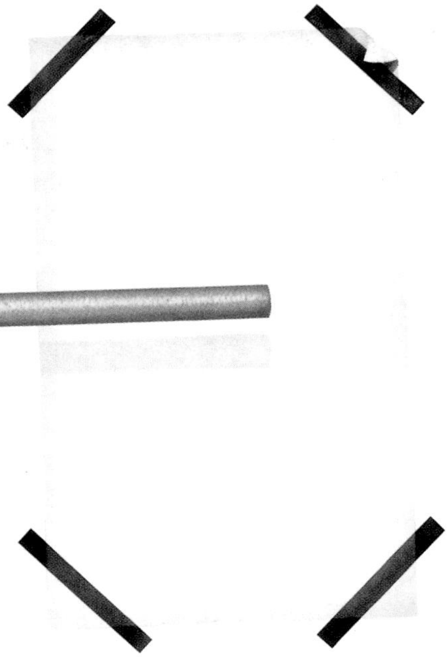

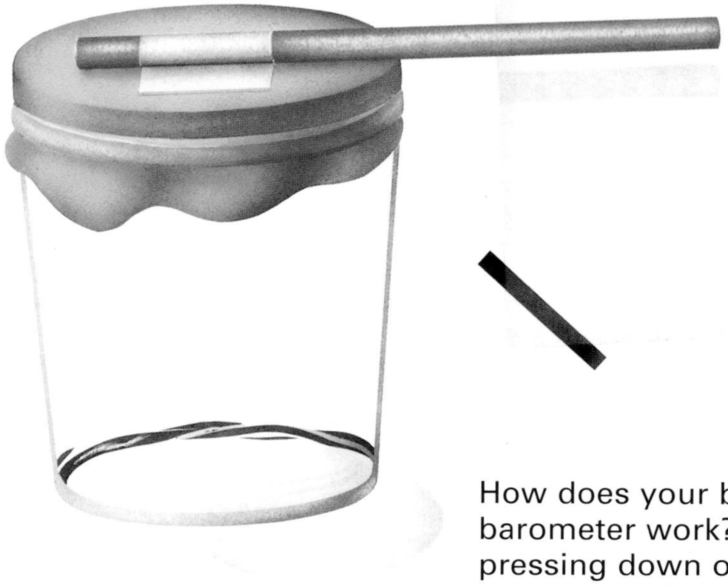

4. Use the pencil to mark the position of the straw end on the paper. Mark the position regularly until there is a change in the weather. The straw should have taken a jump up or down just before the weather changed. Check back and see if it did.

5. For a few more days, mark the position of the straw and add a note about the weather (hot and sunny, cool and rainy, and so on). Can you tell what kind of weather to expect by watching the high and low points?

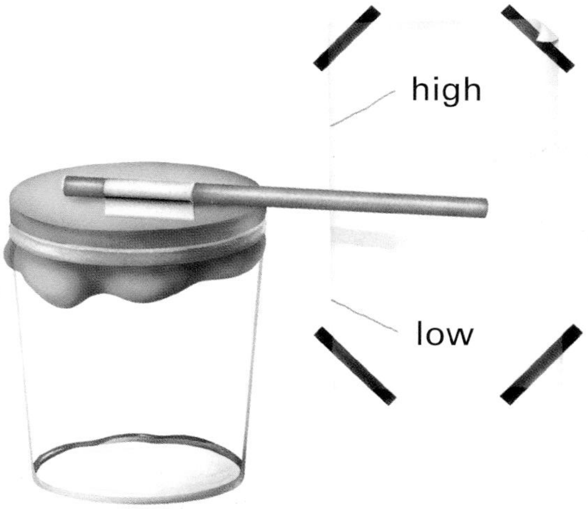

How does your balloon barometer work? Air pressing down on the stretched balloon makes it curve down, which forces the free end of the straw up. The more pressure there is pressing down, the higher the straw points and you can expect sunny skies. The less pressure, the lower the straw points: expect clouds or wet conditions.

It's in the Wind

FaQ

Where does the wind come from?

Long ago, the Japanese thought a god named Fu Jin had a huge bag of wind. If he opened it a little the winds would be gentle; if he opened it wide ... whoosh!

Today, we know there's no wind bag involved when the wind blows. Winds happen when air flows from an area of high pressure to an area of lower pressure.

It's a bit like letting the air out of a balloon. The air in the balloon is under high pressure. When you open the end of the balloon, the air flows into the lower pressure air outside and you make a miniature wind.

What causes high and low pressure areas on Earth? The Sun heats up some areas more than others. The air above these hot spots is warmed, too, and rises.

This rising air forms a low pressure area at the hot spot. The surrounding air flows into this low pressure area, creating wind.

Byte

Ever notice how wind makes a cold day feel even colder? To take into account the wind's chilling effect, people who study weather (meteorologists) talk about "windchill." They have calculated how the combination of wind speed and temperature makes you feel. For example, if the thermometer says –18°C (0°F) and the wind is blowing at 16 km/h (10 m.p.h.), it feels like –30°C (–22°F). Brrrrrr!

FaQ

How far and how long do winds blow?

It depends on whether they're local or global. Local winds may blow for a short distance of up to 500 km (300 mi.). Some, such as the mistral in France, happen only at one time of year. But the big global winds blow long distances all the time. The Earth's spinning makes them flow in different directions.

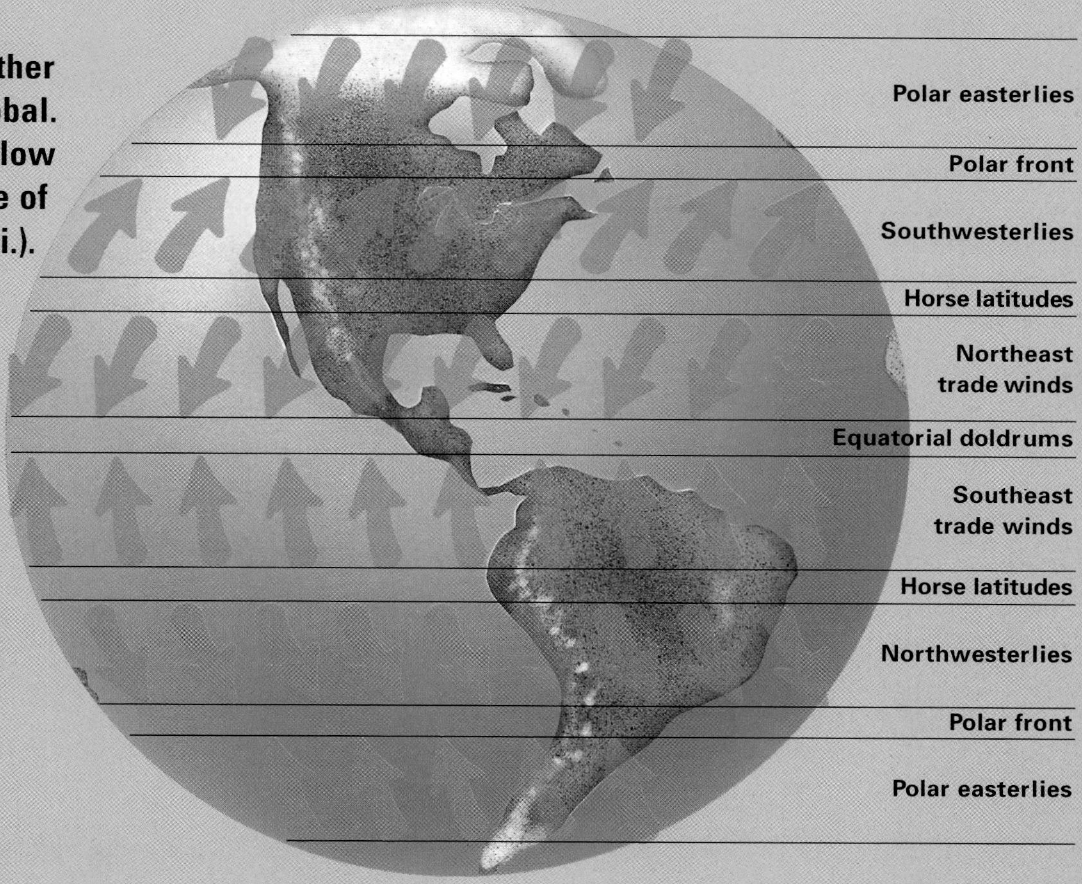

Hold onto Your Hat

FaQ

How can you tell the direction of the wind?

You need a weather vane, sometimes called a wind vane. Knowing where the wind is coming from will tell you a lot about the weather. Here's how to make a weather vane.

You'll need

a felt pen
a square piece of wood
a hammer
2 nails, 7.5 cm (3 in.) long
a cork
a cap from a pen
a feather with a long shaft
a compass
a ruler
glue

1. Use the ruler and felt pen to draw diagonals to find the center point of the piece of wood. Mark the directions North, South, East and West as shown.

2. Hammer one nail partway into the center point. It should stick out about 5 cm (2 in.).

3. Use the other nail to dig a hole in the cork for the pen cap to fit into. If it doesn't fit snugly, glue it in place.

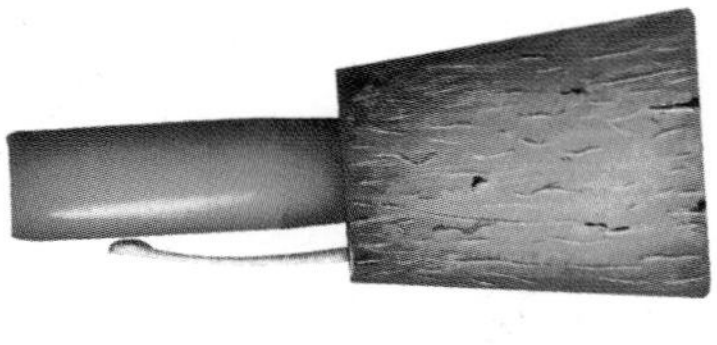

4. Glue the feather across the middle of the cork as shown.

5. Put the pen cap on the nail on the block of wood. Use the compass to line up North on your weather vane with magnetic North.

6. Set the weather vane outside and watch it swivel as it catches the wind. The pointy quill end of the feather will point into the wind and tell you which direction the wind is coming from. For example, if it points South, it's a south wind.

Bytes

- Xlokk, simoom, kwat, bhoot — sound like Martian fast-food? Actually they're winds that blow so regularly in the same place that they've been given names. Can you match each of these winds to the country or continent where it blows? Look at the bottom of the page to see if you are right.

1. Bhoot	A. Asia and Africa
2. Kwat	B. Malta
3. Simoom	C. China
4. Xlokk	D. India

- Hold onto your hat if you visit New Hampshire's Mt. Washington. Winds gusting 372 km/h (231 m.p.h.) have been recorded there, strong enough to rip your hat — and the rest of your clothes — right off.

- Chinooks are hot dry winds that sweep down the eastern slopes of the Rocky Mountains. The word chinook comes from a Native word meaning "snow eater." True to their name, chinooks can "eat" a knee-deep snowfall in just a few hours.

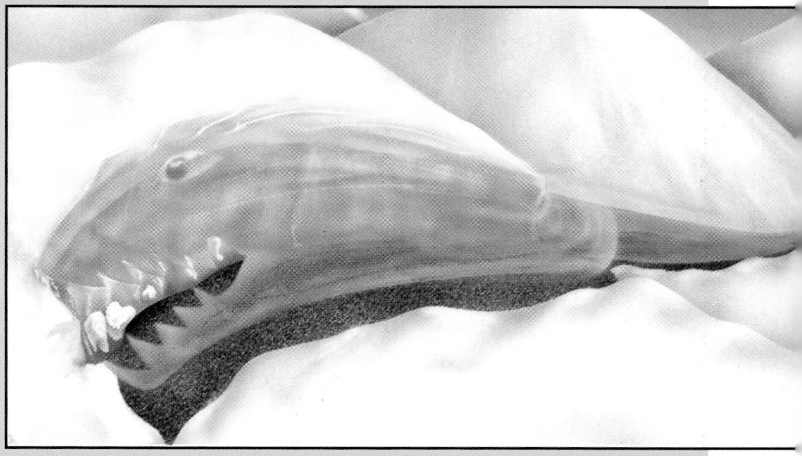

Answers to Byte: 1. D, 2. C, 3. A, 4. B

Put Your Head in the Clouds

FaQ Where do clouds come from?

Clouds in the sky are like a big version of the cloud you make when you breathe out on a very cold day. Water vapor in your warm breath condenses when it hits the cold outside air and sticks to tiny particles in the air. Presto, you've made a cloud.

The same thing happens in the sky. When warm, moist air is cooled, the water vapor in it sticks to floating particles. Millions of tiny cloud droplets are formed. It is these droplets that give clouds their hazy white look. Cloud droplets are minuscule. It would take about a million of them to make an average-sized raindrop.

Byte

A single stratus cloud can cover 1 000 000 sq. km (390 000 sq. mi.). If one of these monster clouds hovered over Texas, it would blanket the whole state and then some.

Why do clouds come in so many different shapes?

A mouse cloud swallows a cat cloud. A dragon cloud turns into a bunny. Become a cloud watcher and you'll spot lots of different shapes and sizes of clouds. Surprisingly, all clouds can be divided into two main types: puffy clouds and flat, layered clouds. They are formed in different ways.

A puffy cloud forms when a small blob of warm, moist air rises and is cooled. This happens when the Sun beams down and warms the Earth, which warms the air close to it, causing the air to rise.

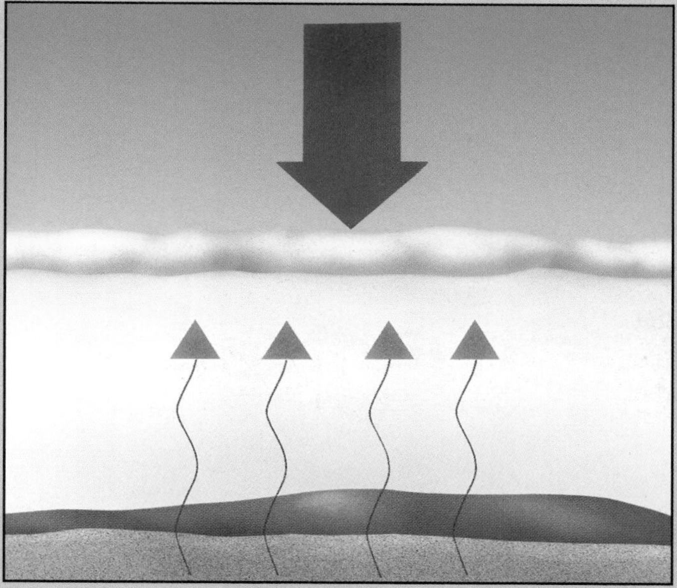

A flat cloud forms when a layer of warm air comes into contact with a layer of cool air. This happens when the warm air rises or when it moves sideways and flows over the cooler air. Clouds form between the two layers.

What is inside a cloud?

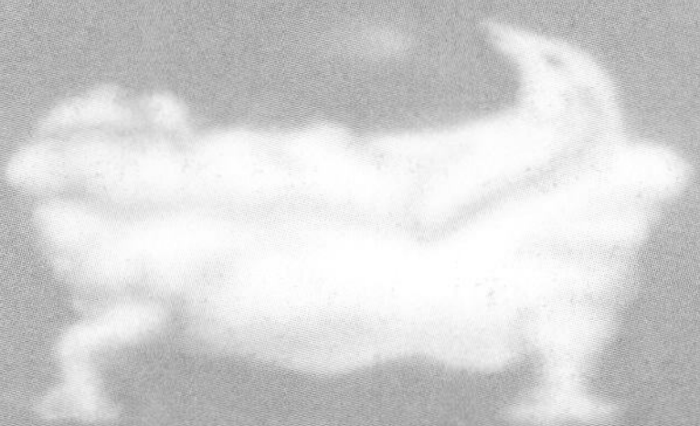

Shut yourself in a steamed-up bathroom and you'll have some idea. Water droplets in the bathroom air are similar to those in a cloud. (However, the air in your bathroom is a lot warmer than the air where real clouds form.) One small puffy white cloud may contain enough water to fill about 1800 bathtubs.

Fogged In

FaQ What is fog?

Walk through fog and you are actually walking through a cloud. Fog forms when moist air close to the ground is cooled. The water vapor in the air sticks to tiny particles and forms droplets just as it does high up in the sky. All those droplets hang in the air close to the ground.

Fogs are common along sea coasts. They happen when moist air from over the water sweeps in over land that is cool. The moisture in the air condenses and suddenly, you're fogged in.

But the places with the most foggy days are hills and mountains. Fog forms when clouds are pushed against a hill or mountain by the wind.

FaQ What is smog?

Smog may look like fog, but don't be fooled. Smog is a mixture of pollutants and water droplets. It forms when chemical pollutants are pumped into the air out of car exhausts and factory chimneys.

In the atmosphere, the pollutants are changed by the Sun's light energy into substances that are harmful to people's health and the environment. This is called photochemical smog — "photo" comes the Greek word meaning "light."

Most big cities broadcast smog alerts or air quality ratings to warn residents with asthma and other breathing problems to stay indoors, so that their lungs won't be irritated.

FAQ

How can you find out what's in the air?

Forest fire soot, plant pollen, sea salt, volcanic dust, dirt and human additions such as pollutants from burning gasoline and other fossil fuels are all in the air you breathe. Achooo! It's enough to make you sneeze. Or is it? Here's how to find out how much gunk is in the air you're breathing.

You'll need

a table knife
petroleum jelly
(available at drugstores)
index cards
a jar
tape

1. Use the table knife to smear a thin layer of petroleum jelly on the index card, but not on the short edges.

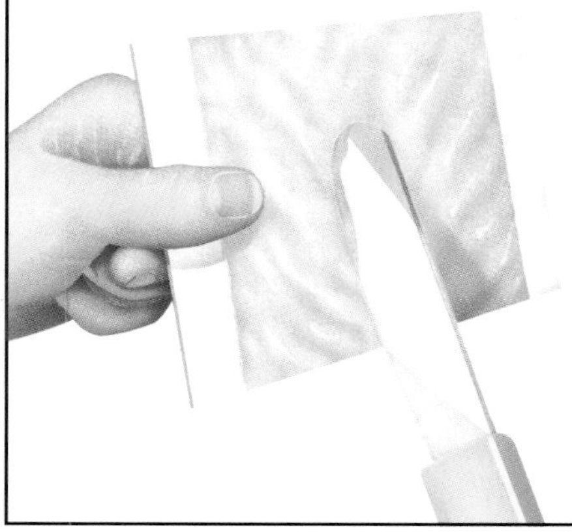

2. Tape the card around the jar as shown.

3. Place the jar outdoors, card side up. Prop it with stones, so that it can't roll around. Leave it for 24 hours, then check how much stuff has collected on the card.

4. Try collecting particles in different places: indoors, beside a busy road (be careful), in your school yard. Use a freshly coated index card for every new place. Where is there the most stuff in the air? The least?

Byte

In a big city, a thimbleful of air may contain more than 100 000 particles. Even at the North Pole there are about 300 particles in the same very small amount of air. Winds carry particles and pollution from one part of the globe to another.

It's Raining, It's Snowing

FaQ

Can you tell if rain or snow is on the way?

A dark cloud in summer means you'd better get out your umbrella. In winter, pull on your snow boots. Dark clouds contain lots of cloud droplets, maybe even ice crystals. That means rain or snow — weather watchers call it "precipitation" — is forming.

Although rain and snow feel very different, they're actually close cousins. In North America, they both often begin as ice crystals up in a cloud. (These ice crystals form when water vapor freezes onto particles in the air or when tiny water droplets freeze.) When the ice crystals become too heavy to stay up, they begin to fall. Now they are called snow crystals. Snow crystals can grow as more water vapor sticks to them or as they collect cloud droplets when they fall.

If the air is cold all the way down to the ground, the snow crystals stay frozen. Sometimes they join together to make snowflakes and we get snow on the ground. If the snow crystals go through warm air on their way down, they melt and fall as raindrops. Rain or snow — they both start out the same.

In warmer parts of the Earth, such as around the equator, ice crystals may not form. Instead, cloud droplets bump together to form raindrops. Time to get out your umbrella!

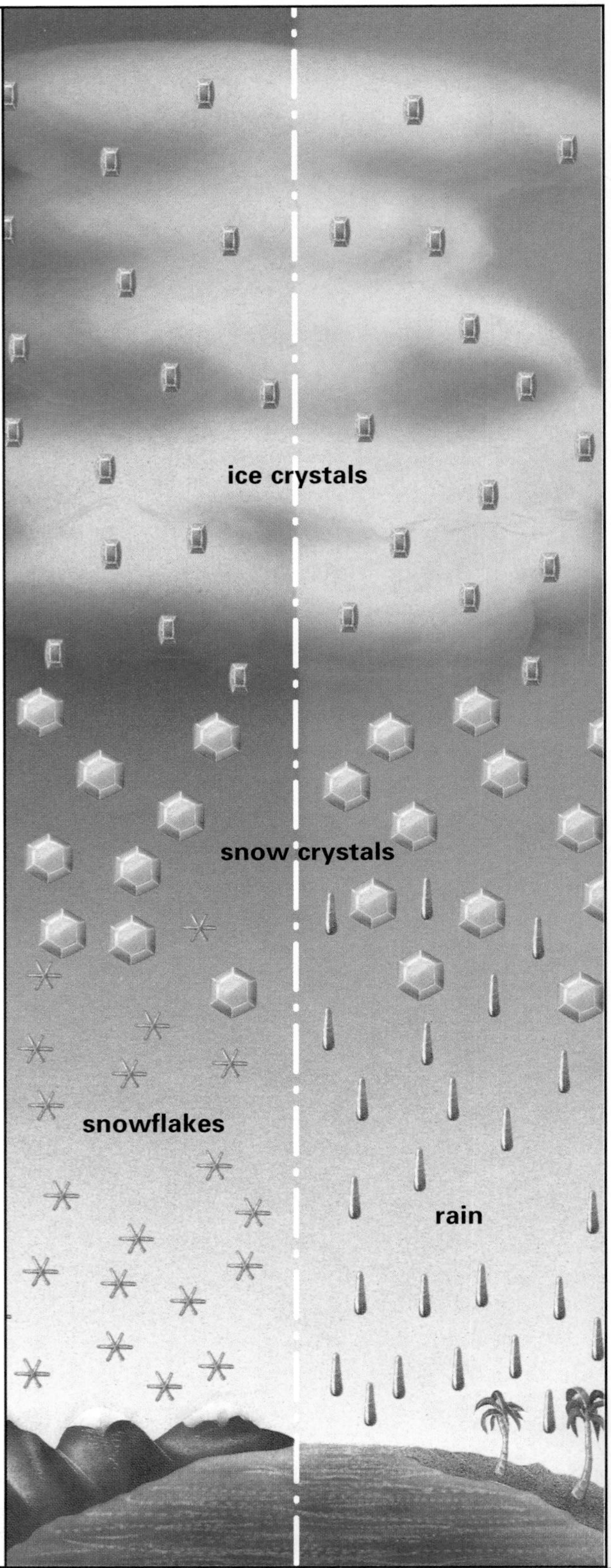

Byte

What's green and red and falls from the sky? Green rain and red snow. Green rain fell over Moscow on May 5, 1987. And red snow fell over northern Italy on October 14, 1755. The color comes from pollen, dirt or other particles in the air carried down to the ground by the precipitation.

FaQ

How does water get up into the clouds?

The water in clouds that becomes snow or rain comes from oceans, lakes, rivers, ponds and even puddles. The Sun heats up the water and turns it from a liquid (water) to a gas (water vapor). This process is called "evaporation." The water vapor floats up into the sky, cools and turns back into a liquid. This is known as "condensation." Eventually rain or snow falls from the clouds and the water ends up back on Earth.

Round and round the water goes — up into the sky and back down again in a cycle that never ends. That's why it's called the "water cycle." Amazingly, the puddle you splashed through today may be raining back down on you next week. Even more amazing, the water that showered the dinosaurs millions of years ago may soak you tomorrow.

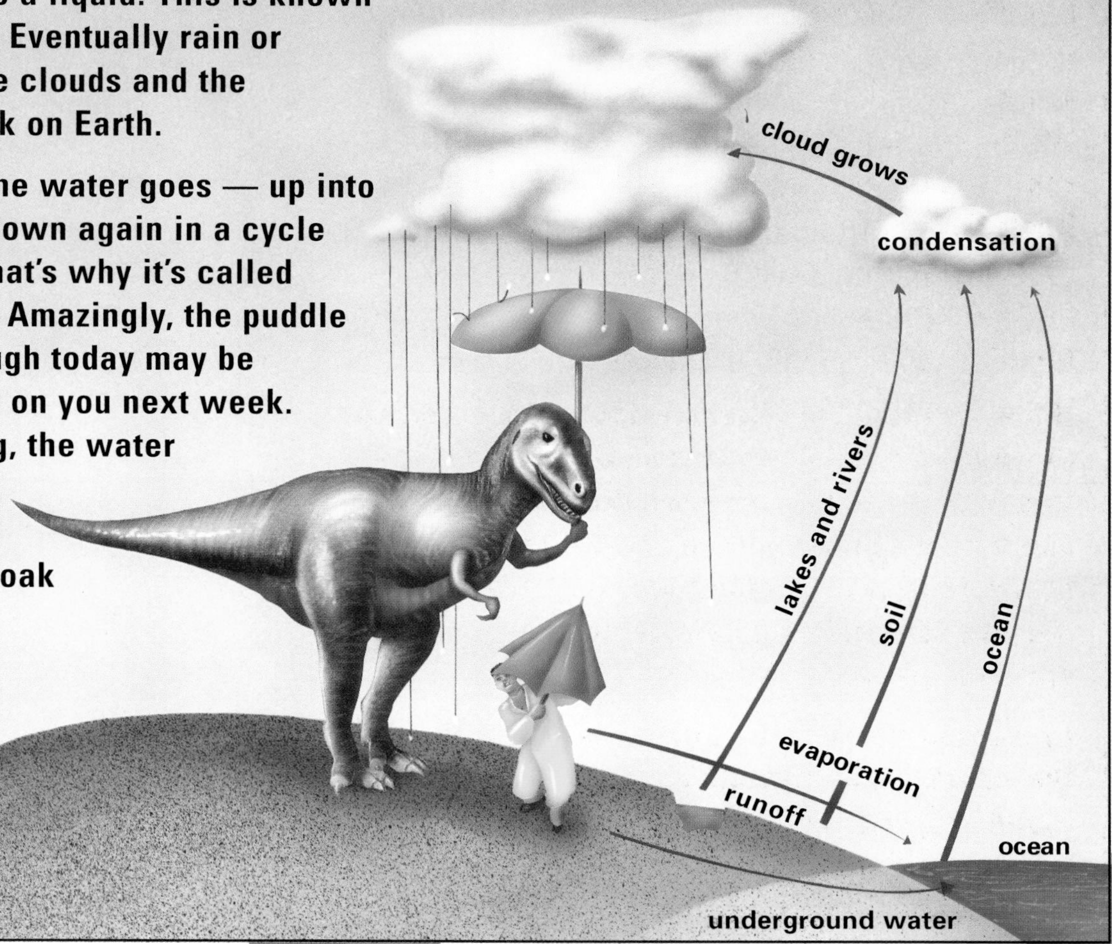

Rain, Rain, Go Away

FaQ What is acid rain?

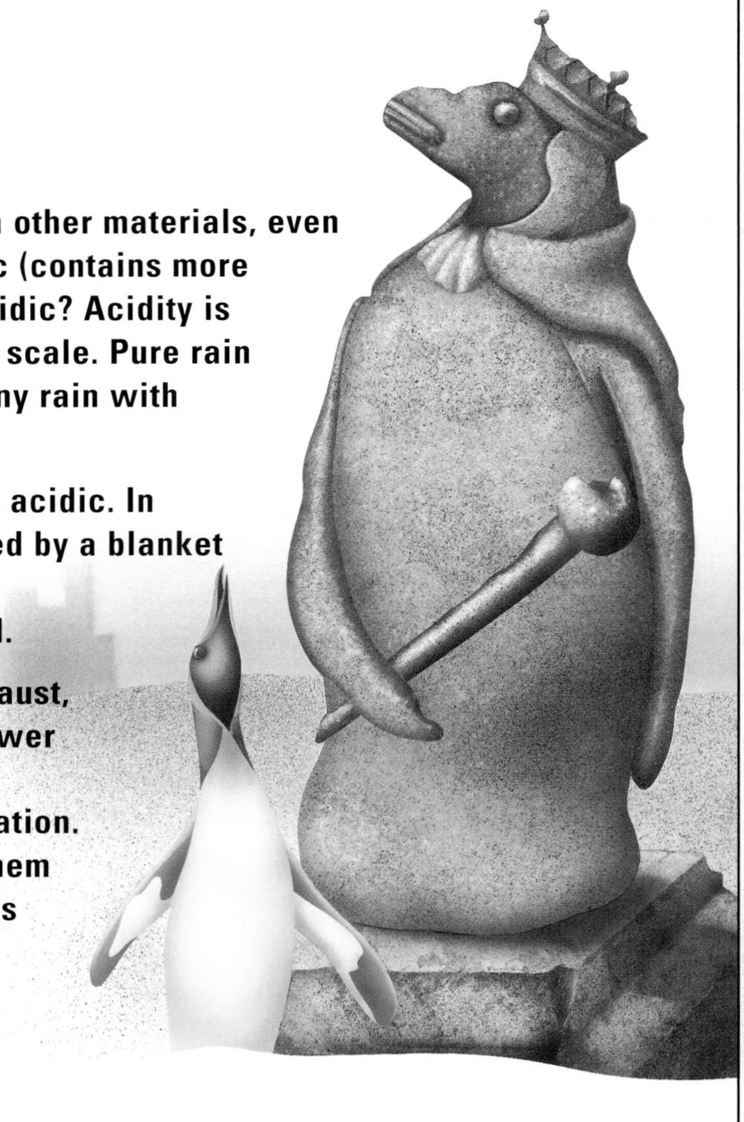

An acid is a chemical that can break down other materials, even metals. Acid rain is rain that is more acidic (contains more acid) than normal rain. How much more acidic? Acidity is measured using a system known as the pH scale. Pure rain has a pH of 5.6, for example. Acid rain is any rain with a pH lower than 5.6.

Snow, sleet, dew and even fog can also be acidic. In December 1982, Los Angeles was smothered by a blanket of acid fog that measured 1.7, the most acidic weather phenomenon ever recorded.

The acid comes from chemicals in car exhaust, industry smokestacks and coal-burning power plants. These are pumped into the air and eventually fall back down as acid precipitation. Acid snow or rain falls on lakes, making them too acidic for fish and other wildlife. It falls on crops and forests, damaging some. It covers buildings, eating away stonework and corroding pipes. It can even dissolve the nose off a statue.

FaQ Are raindrops shaped like teardrops?

No — they're shaped like hamburger buns. As they fall, air pressure on the underside flattens the bottom slightly.

FaQ

How big are raindrops?

Most raindrops are small because big ones usually break apart as they fall. Even the world's biggest raindrop, which fell near Hilo, Hawaii, measured only 8 mm (1/3 in.) across. That's smaller than your baby fingernail. How big a raindrop can you catch?

You'll need

a shoe box lid
flour
a ruler
a fine mesh sieve
a bowl

1. Fill the lid with flour. Use the ruler to smooth the top so that it's level.

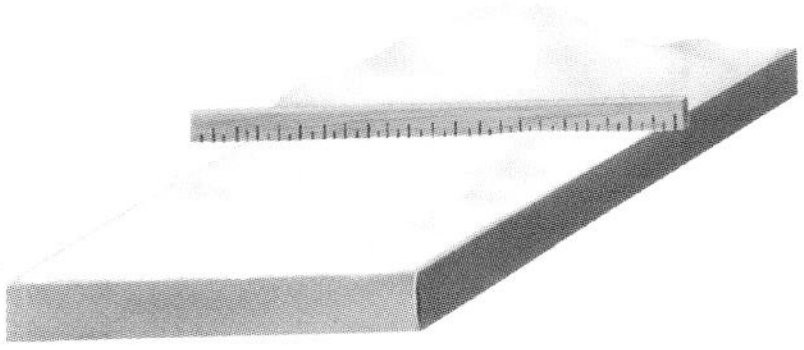

2. When it rains, hold the lid out in the rain until about 20 raindrops have fallen into the flour. Bring the lid inside.

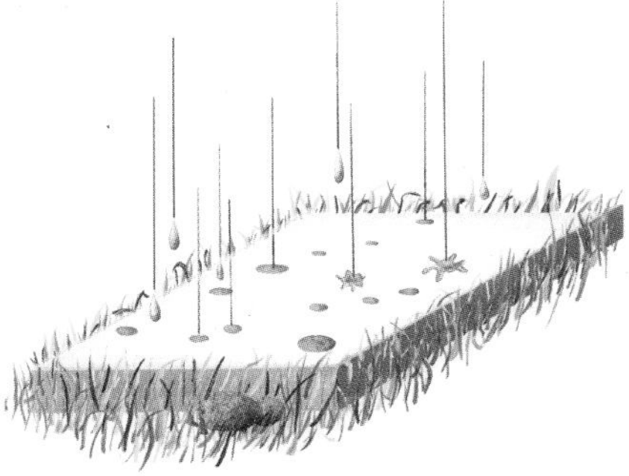

3. Set the sieve over the bowl. Carefully pour the flour from the lid into the bowl. Shake the sieve gently.

4. The little lumps left behind in the sieve are preserved raindrops. Gently dump them out onto a table and measure them.

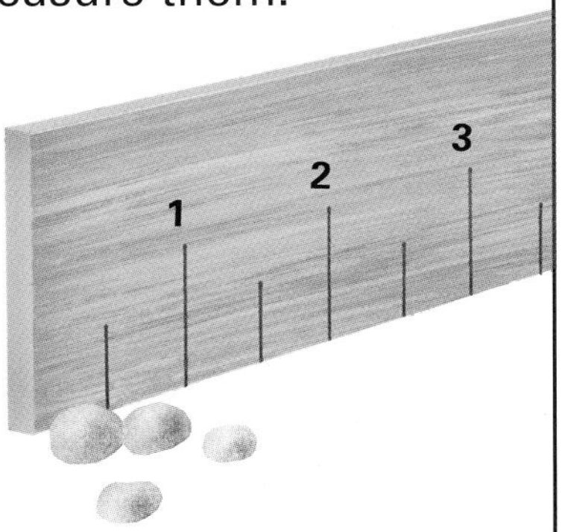

FaQ

What causes rainbows?

People used to think there was a pot of gold at the end of the rainbow. That's just a legend, but there is something magical about rainbows.

They form when sunlight strikes raindrops in the air and is split into bands of colors. You see these bands as an arc in the sky. The colors are always in the same order: red, orange, yellow, green, blue, indigo and violet. If you want to remember the order, use this sentence as a memory aid: Ratting On Your Goofy Brother Is Vile.

Sometimes a double rainbow forms— one inside the other. The outside rainbow is fainter and the colors are in the reverse order.

Let It Snow

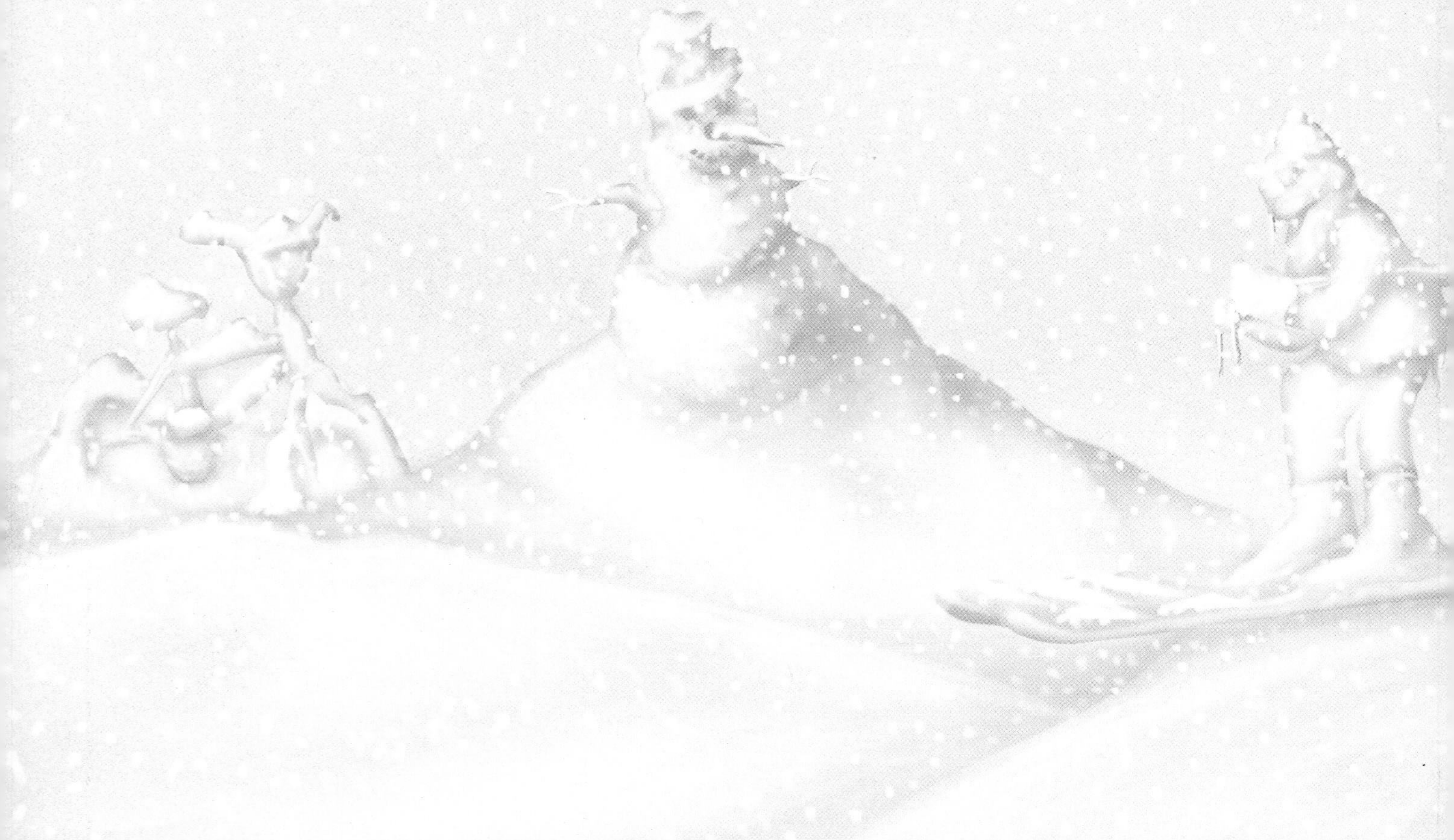

FaQ

Is it ever too cold to snow?

Even if it's cold enough to make a penguin shiver, don't put away your snow shovel. It's never too cold to snow. However, when the temperature plummets, there's less water vapor in the air and it's harder for snowflakes to form. So there's less snow to shovel than when it's slightly warmer.

FaQ

Do all snowflakes look like this?

No, all snowflakes are different because they are made up of snow crystals that combine in different ways. There are six main snow crystal shapes (see page 39). The snowflakes that you see are assembled out of two or more of these snowflake "building blocks." Next time it snows, try catching a snowflake and taking a close look at it.

You'll need

a small, clean piece of glass, such as a microscope slide

spray-on clear plastic lacquer (available at hardware or craft stores)

tweezers

a magnifying glass or microscope (optional)

1. Put the glass and lacquer into the freezer and let them cool completely — overnight, if possible.

2. When it's snowing, use the tweezers to remove the glass from the freezer. (Try not to let the glass get warm.) Spray a thin coating of lacquer on one side and tilt the glass to get rid of any extra lacquer.

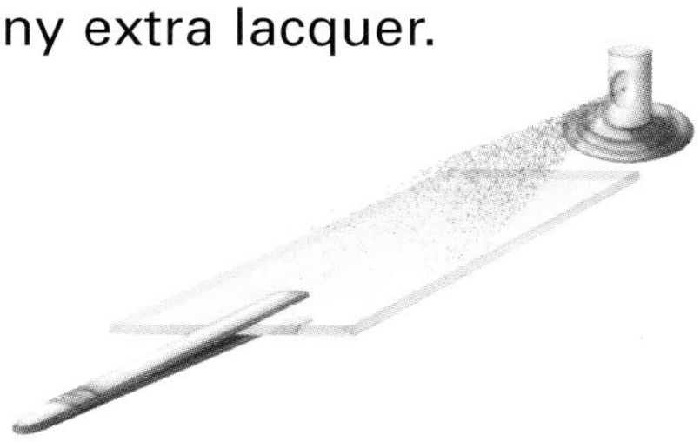

3. Immediately put the glass outside, lacquer side up, and wait till a snowflake lands on it.

4. Using the tweezers, put the glass in a protected area outside, where no more flakes will fall on it. Leave it for one hour.

5. Bring the glass inside and use a magnifying glass or a microscope, if you have one, to look at the impression the snowflake made.

Bytes

- The world's largest snowflake was 38 cm (15 in.) in diameter, bigger than a dinner plate.
- Scientists estimate that a single snowstorm can drop 36 million tonnes (40 million tons) of snow.

Freezing Rain, Sleet, Hail, Frost and Dew

FaQ

What is the difference between freezing rain and sleet?

You step out the door and plant a foot on the sidewalk. Before you can say "winter wonderland," you're flat on your back seeing stars. Poor you. You're a victim of freezing rain or sleet. But which one?

Freezing rain is rain that freezes when it hits the ground. The result: instant skating rink. Branches and wires sag and snap under the weight of the ice. When an ice storm hit eastern Canada and the northeastern U.S. in 1998, power poles toppled and electrical wires snapped, leaving some people without heat or light for weeks.

Sleet (also called "ice pellets") is the name given to frozen raindrops, snow encased in ice or partially melted snowflakes. Sleet doesn't stick to things the way freezing rain does, but it can still make for a walk on the wild side.

FaQ: What causes frost?

It's not Jack Frost who decorates the world white in winter. Frost happens when water vapor in the air strikes something cold, such as a window, tree branch or power line. The water vapor settles onto tiny bits of dirt or scratches in the glass and freezes into crystals. The crystal structure does the rest, interlocking to form beautiful patterns. Jack Frost couldn't do it better.

FaQ: What is dew?

Dew is a warm-weather cousin of frost. On summer nights, water vapor in the air near the ground condenses onto cool objects such as grass and spiderwebs. When you wake up, the world is dotted with tiny drops of water.

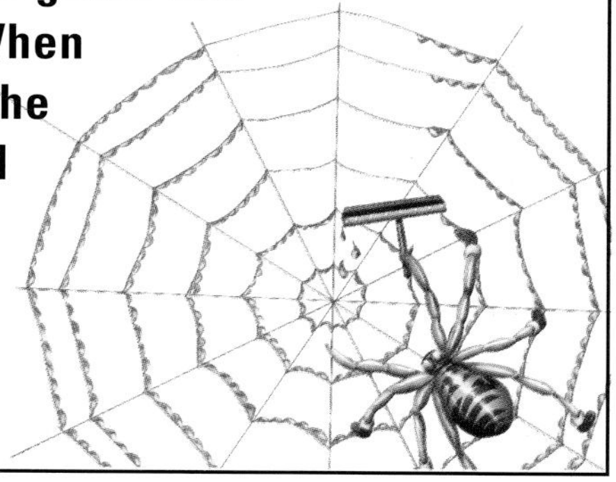

FaQ: How does hail form?

Hail starts out as tiny ice crystals up in a cloud. As these ice crystals grow, they usually fall as snow or rain. But sometimes the ice crystals are trapped inside a big cloud and are carried up and down. If this happens over and over, the ice crystals may collect layer upon layer of ice. Now they are hailstones and are so heavy they fall.

The more layers hail has, the bigger it is — and the bigger the crash when it hits the ground. On September 3, 1979, a hailstone bigger than a cantaloupe smashed into the town of Coffeyville, Kansas. Ouch!

Thunder and Lightning

FaQ What is a thunderstorm?

The sky darkens as towering clouds churn overhead. Rain falls, whipped by the wind. Lightning flashes and thunder booms. Take cover — it's a thunderstorm, the most dangerous kind of rainstorm.

Thunderstorms start when fast-rising, warm, moist air cools and forms a cloud that grows taller and taller until it is a towering column. Air currents build and churn within the thundercloud. Downdrafts and updrafts battle it out. Some downdrafts roar out the bottom of the cloud, causing high winds. Rain forms and starts to fall. Soon the sky is streaked with lightning and split with cracks of thunder.

FaQ

What causes thunder and lightning?

Have you ever shocked a friend by rubbing your feet on a carpet and then touching him? Rubbing your feet gives you an electrical charge. The shock happens when electricity jumps between electrically charged you and your uncharged friend.

Much the same thing happens during a thunderstorm. Winds and rain act like the carpet, creating an electrical charge at the bottom of the cloud. Electricity zaps to the ground below. What you see as a single stroke of lightning is actually a super-fast zapping from the cloud to the ground and back to the cloud again, three or four times.

Lightning is sizzling hot. As it streaks down, it instantly heats the air around it, making the air suddenly expand. The rapid expansion sends out shock waves that travel through the air and into your ear. Rumble, kaboom. It's thunder!

FaQ

Can you survive getting hit by lightning?

Just ask Roy "Dooms" Sullivan. He was struck by lightning seven times. Mr. Sullivan was lucky to survive — lightning can kill. If you'd like a close encounter with lightning that's safe, try making some ... in your mouth. All you need are some wintergreen-flavored hard candies. Take a mirror into a dark room or closet. Chew on the candy with your mouth open and watch your mouth in the mirror. Do you see flashes of light?

Chewing rips apart the sugar crystals, making islands of candy that have different electrical charges. Sparks of electricity jump between the islands, like a mini-lightning bolt.

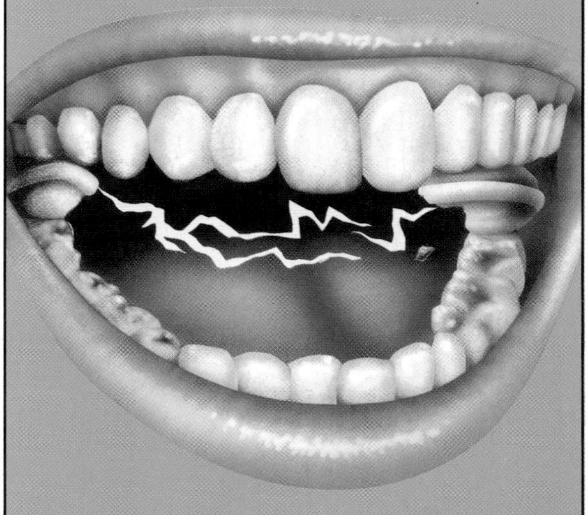

Tornadoes, Monsoons and El Niño

FaQ

What are tornadoes?

A long tube of swirling wind snakes out of a thundercloud. As it touches the ground it leaves a path of debris behind it, flipping cars upside down, flattening houses and ripping trees out by their roots.

Tornadoes sometimes form during thunderstorms. Updrafts in the thundercloud are sent spinning by higher level winds, much as you can start water in a bath spiraling just by swirling your hand at the surface. The spinning winds form a tube that extends below the thundercloud.

An average-sized tornado is about 225 m (250 yd.) across, or bigger than two football fields end to end. Its rotating winds can travel faster than 400 km/h (250 m.p.h.). The hole in the center is a low pressure area. As the tornado storms across fields and towns, it rips objects to shreds and sucks them up into the air like a vacuum cleaner gone mad.

Tornadoes can be deadly destructive or strangely delicate. A tornado in 1942 harvested a farmer's potato crop in Killarney, Manitoba. In 1951 a tornado blowing in Scottsbluff, Nebraska, plucked the feathers off a chicken without harming it.

FaQ What is a monsoon?

Every summer in India, winds that usually flow out to sea shift direction to bring cool, moist air from the ocean over the land. There the air dumps its moisture. This is a monsoon — a wind that flows from the ocean over land and brings heavy rains.

The monsoon is eagerly awaited because it means an end to the dry season. It brings so much rain to Cherrapunji, in northern India, that the city holds the world's record for the most rainfall — 2646.17 cm (1041-8/10 in.) in just one year. That would be enough to submerge a seven-story building.

Monsoons begin when the air above the land and the water have different temperatures. The warmer air starts to rise and cooler air flows in. The monsoon begins.

FaQ What is El Niño?

No snow in Canada but mounds of it in Mexico? Blame it on El Niño. It's a warming of the ocean off Peru and Ecuador that occurs late in December some years. The warmed ocean adds heat and moisture to the atmosphere, starting a chain reaction that shakes up Earth's normal weather patterns. A cooling of the ocean in this area can occur, too. It's called La Niña and it can bring its own scrambled weather.

Hurricane!

FaQ

What is a hurricane?

Hurricanes (also known as typhoons or cyclones) are huge storms of high-speed, spiraling winds. Often there is a calm area in the middle of the storm called the "eye." To earn the name hurricane, a storm must have winds of at least 119 km/h (74 m.p.h.) that blow for long periods, not just short gusts.

FaQ

How do hurricanes form?

A hurricane starts out as an ordinary storm over warm ocean waters. But as it absorbs heat and water from the ocean below, it grows bigger and bigger. An average hurricane is about 600 km (375 mi.) across. That's the distance from New York City to Norfolk, Virginia.

The huge, spiraling storm slowly starts to move, carried westward by the prevailing winds in the region. At sea, boats are tossed around like toys. If the hurricane hits land it can destroy whole communities. Violent winds rip buildings apart and uproot trees and power lines. Rain lashes down, causing flooding.

Then suddenly there is calm as the eye of the storm — the doughnut hole in the middle — passes over. Winds and rain stop. Exhausted birds that have been fighting the winds get a rest. But after the eye of the storm passes by, watch out. The winds roar and the rains pour down again.

Hurricanes gradually weaken as they pass over land or cool, northerly waters. Without the warm ocean water to feed on, they cannot survive. The average hurricane only lives for about nine days, but in 1971 Hurricane Ginger just wouldn't die. It lasted for 22 days.

Bytes

- The eye of a hurricane is on average 30 km (18 1/2 mi.) across. How big is that? Imagine 425 jumbo jets parked end to end.
- Hurricanes are named according to the letters of the alphabet. A name beginning with A is given to the first hurricane of the year, B to the second and so on. Male and female names alternate. Can you figure out how many hurricanes there were in 1996 before Hurricane Fran swept along the east coast of North America?

Weather or Not?

FaQ

Why does the Earth warm up or cool down?

Weather changes from day to day. Climate is an average of the weather over many years and changes very slowly.

If the climate where you live is cold, you may get a few warm days in winter but most days will be cold.

FaQ

Has Earth's climate always been the way it is today?

No. There have been periods of global cooling, when Earth's average temperature fell. Cooling led to ice ages long ago. At other times the climate was much warmer or wetter than it is today. For example, about 20 000 years ago, northern Canada was warm enough for camel-like animals.

FaQ

Why does the Earth warm up or cool down?

How warm or cool Earth becomes depends on how much solar energy we get from the Sun. No one is sure why the amount varies, but here are some theories. Long ago, a period of intense sunspot activity may have meant more solar energy, causing warming. Or the amount of solar energy may also vary as a result of Earth's tilt and orbit, which both change over time. Another theory is that meteors may have hit Earth, pumping dust into the atmosphere and blocking the Sun's warmth. Anything that changes the solar energy reaching Earth also changes Earth's climate.

Today there is another cause — human activity. By burning coal, oil and natural gas in factories, homes and cars, we are adding "greenhouse gases" to the atmosphere. These gases act like the glass in a greenhouse and trap the Sun's warmth near Earth. The result: we may experience global warming.

FaQ

What will the weather be like if there is global warming?

Greenhouse gases do not let the extra heat of the Sun's radiant energy escape into space. The gases trap the heat near the Earth's surface.

Even a slight warming could be big trouble. There could be more severe storms and periods of drought. Wet areas could become dry and vice versa. Food production and forests could be disrupted, causing problems for people and wildlife.

How can global warming be stopped? By using energy wisely and burning fewer fossil fuels. This would reduce the greenhouse gases that cause global warming. For example, by buying only things that you really need, you can cut down on the fossil fuels it takes to produce stuff. And by bicycling instead of being driven places, you help reduce the fossil fuels being pumped into the atmosphere.

Byte

The last ice age lasted from the 1500s to the mid 1800s. It was called the Little Ice Age and it was so cold that people in Europe needed warmer clothes. Beaver hats became popular and this led to a boom in the fur trade, which brought many European explorers and settlers to Canada.

What Will the  Weather Be Like?

FaQ How can I monitor the weather where I live?

Set up your own weather station using the weather equipment in this book. Use the barometer from page 9 to predict changes in the weather. Make the weather vane on page 12 to find out the wind direction. Add an outdoor thermometer to keep track of the temperature. And set up this rain gauge to monitor precipitation.

You'll need

a glass with straight sides
a ruler
clear tape

1. Hold the glass at eye level. Position the ruler as shown. (You want to measure what's in the glass — not the bottom of the glass, too.) Tape the ruler in place.

2. Put your rain gauge outside on a flat surface. After a rainfall, record how much rain fell. Check your local weather forecast to find out the official rainfall. Did the same amount of rain fall in your neighborhood?

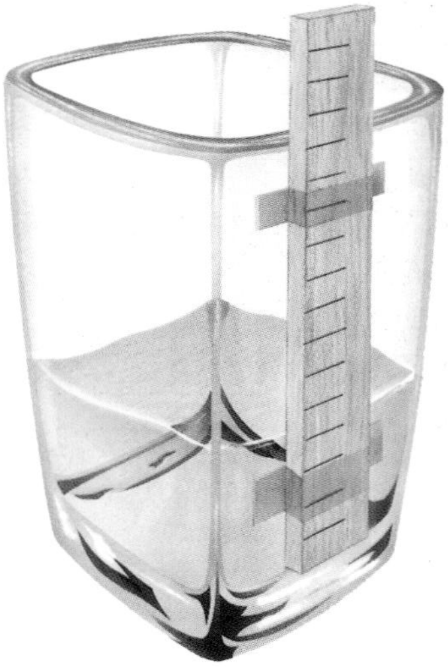

FaQ Why do people try to predict the weather?

Fishers, farmers and airline pilots depend on weather reports for their work. Many other people use hurricane, tornado and other weather warnings to get out of the way of approaching storms. Forecasting the weather saves money and lives. And predicting longer-term climate change can allow people to make adjustments before it is too late. We can't change the weather, but we can learn to live with it by learning about it.

FaQ

How do people know what the weather will be like in the future?

Tomorrow's weather is fairly easy to predict. Next week's weather is trickier, and next month's is almost impossible. Winds, ocean currents, air masses, storms — so many things combine that long-range weather is, well, unpredictable.

But meteorologists don't give up. They gather information on the weather from instruments on the ground and out in space. Then these weather watchers use computers to analyze the information and try to predict whether you should haul out your skateboard — or your ice skates.

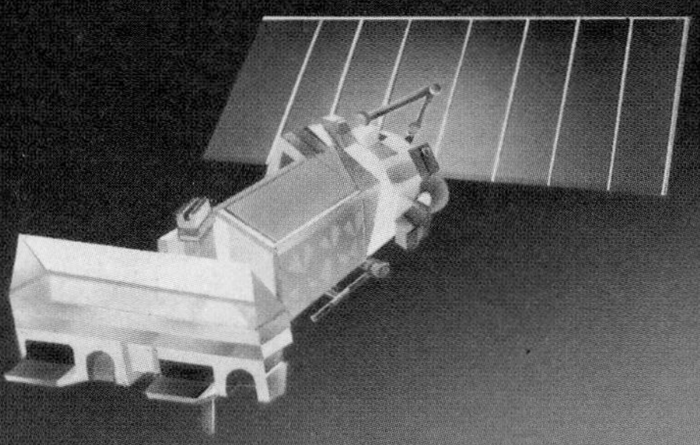

Seven weather satellites orbit Earth and send back data on cloud cover, storms and other large-scale weather systems. Watch weather reports on TV and you'll see the pictures of clouds moving over your area that these weather satellites provide.

Helium-filled weather balloons carry equipment that measures the temperature, air pressure and humidity (moisture in the air). They beam data to operators on the ground until the balloons float so high that — bam! — they burst.

Radar stations on Earth transmit radio beams that can detect building thunderstorms and other severe weather.

On the ground, the temperature, wind and precipitation are measured daily. Sometimes people record these measurements; other times automated weather stations do the work.

Extreme Weather

Pull on your parka, get out your umbrella and don't forget your bathing suit. You're about to experience the wettest, hottest and downright weirdest weather anywhere on earth.

Duck!

The world's heaviest hailstones fell in Bangladesh on April 14, 1986. One of the monsters weighed 1 kg ($2\frac{1}{4}$ lb.), as much as a small bag of flour.

Sweat or shiver?

In a single day the temperature difference between the North and South Poles can be as much as 82°C (180°F).

Splash!

July 4, 1956, wasn't a day for picnics in Unionville, Maryland. That's the day they set a world record for the heaviest rainfall in one minute — 31 mm ($1\frac{1}{4}$ in.) of rain. If it had rained that hard for a whole hour, the water would have been over your head.

Gasp!

You'd be yearning for rain if you lived in Arica, Chile. Not so much as a drop of rain was recorded there for 14 years in a row.

Zap!

Thunderstorm fans should plan a visit to Bogor, Indonesia. It holds the world record for number of thunderstorm days in a year — 322. That means there were only 43 days that year when they *didn't* have thunderstorms.

Whew!

Feeling chilly? You might want to move to Marble Bar, Australia. They had a record-breaking hot spell of temperatures higher than 38°C (100°F). How long did it last? A scorching 162 days straight.

Hello? Hello?

In a fog? You'd feel right at home in the world's foggiest place — Old Glory Mountain in British Columbia. It's foggy there an average of 226 days a year.

Other weather records

Hottest place on Earth, see page 6

Coldest place on Earth, see page 6

Largest snowflake, see page 23

Most rainfall in one year, see page 29

Glossary

acid rain: rain that has a pH lower than 5.6, making it more acidic than normal rain

air mass: a large body of air with fairly uniform temperature and humidity

air pressure: the force that air exerts

atmosphere: the blanket of air that surrounds Earth

barometer: a device that measures air pressure and predicts changes in the weather

climate: the pattern of weather in an area over a long period of time

cloud: a mass of very tiny water droplets, called cloud droplets, in the sky

condensation: the change from gas to liquid. Water vapor condenses into liquid water.

crystal: a solid with regular surfaces and structure

dew: water in the air that condenses on cool objects near the ground

evaporation: the change from liquid to gas. Liquid water evaporates and becomes water vapor.

fog: a cloud of water droplets that forms near the ground

freezing rain: rain that freezes when it hits the ground

frost: ice crystals that form on objects in cold weather

global warming: the increase in Earth's average temperature

greenhouse gases: gases that trap some of the Sun's heat close to Earth's surface, like the glass in a greenhouse

hail: ice crystals surrounded by layers of ice

humidity: moisture in the air

hurricane: a severe storm of spiraling winds that starts over the Atlantic Ocean

lightning: an electrical charge that travels between a cloud and the ground or between clouds

meteorologist: a scientist who studies weather

monsoon: a flow of air from the ocean to the land that brings rain

precipitation: rain, snow and other forms of water or ice that fall from clouds

rain: precipitation that falls in the form of liquid water

sleet: small ice pellets

smog: a fog-like mixture of pollutants, particles and water droplets

snow: solid precipitation that falls in the form of white ice crystals

thunder: the shock waves from rapidly expanding air caused by heating as lightning passes through it. The rapid expansion produces a bang or rumble.

tornado: a swirling funnel of air that descends from a cloud and can cause severe damage

water cycle: the movement of water as it evaporates from lakes, rivers, soil and oceans, rises into the atmosphere, condenses and falls as precipitation

water vapor: water in a gas-like form

weather: the changes in atmospheric conditions that happen day to day

wind: the flow of air from an area of high pressure to an area of lower pressure

Cloud Chart

Here are some common types of clouds. On most days you can see two or more types of clouds in the sky at the same time.

Cirrus

These wispy, white clouds form high in the sky where it is cold. They are made of ice crystals, rather than tiny droplets of water like most clouds.

Cumulus

White and puffy with flat bases and rounded tops, cumulus clouds often signal good weather, especially when they form in the afternoon.

Cirrostratus (at sunset)

Like many clouds, these clouds are a mixture of two types. They combine the height of cirrus clouds with the layering of stratus clouds. True stratus clouds are gray sheets of cloud relatively close to the ground.

Cumulonimbus

If clouds have "nimbus" as part of their name, they are dark gray or purple and are probably rain clouds. Cumulonimbus clouds are very tall and can look as if they've been blown sideways.

Altocumulus

Clouds with "alto" at the start of their name are middle-level clouds. This means they form higher in the sky than ordinary cumulus clouds but not as high as cirrus clouds.

Snow Chart

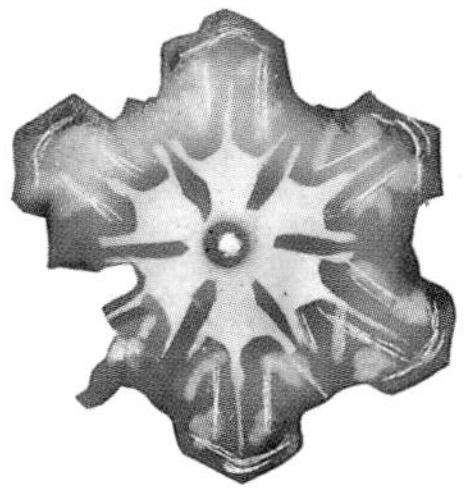

Plate

Stellar

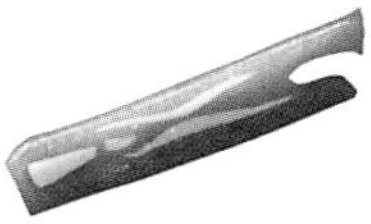

Column

Needle

Spatial dendrite

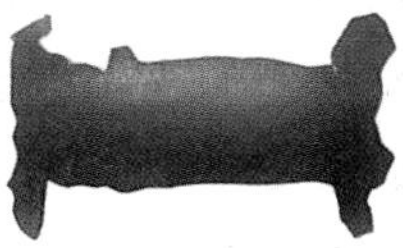

Capped column

Index